GROWING COLORS

BRUCE McMILLAN

FOR CHELSEA

LOTHROP, LEE & SHEPARD BOOKS · NEW YORK

Library of Congress Cataloging in Publication Data McMillan, Bruce. Growing colors. Summary: Photographs of green peas, yellow corn, red potatoes, purple beans, and other fruits and vegetab es illustrate the many colors of nature. 1. Color—Juvenile literature. 2. Vegetables—Color—Juvenile literature.   3. Fruit—Color—Juvenile literature.   [1. Color. 2. Vegetables. 3. Fruit] I. Title.   QC495.5.M38 1988 535.6 88-2767
ISBN 0-688-07844-3   ISBN 0-688-07845-1 (lib. bdg.)

RED

3

ORANGE

YELLOW

GREEN

BLUE

PURPLE

ORANGE

BROWN

WHITE

PURPLE

23

YELLOW

BLACK

THE FRUITS & VEGETABLES

RED RASPBERRIES

ORANGE CARROTS

YELLOW SUMMER SQUASH

GREEN PEAS

BLUE BLUEBERRIES

PURPLE BEANS

TAN CANTALOUPES

ORANGE APRICOTS

BROWN PEPPERS

WHITE ONIONS

PURPLE PLUMS

YELLOW CORN

RED POTATOES

BLACK BLACKBERRIES

This book is about color in nature. It is a color book and also a nature teaching tool that shows how fruits and vegetables grow in, on, or above the ground. In addition to green peas, orange carrots, yellow corn, and other familiar fruit and vegetable color associations, readers are introduced to less-known color varieties, such as purple beans, red potatoes, and brown peppers. Most fruits and vegetables grow in a wide variety of colors, as is true of the peppers shown above.

All colors in the photographs are as they were found in nature. Colors in nature are always at their best when wet from rain. To bring out the full existing colors, a photographer-made shower was produced with a portable water sprayer. The lighting was natural sun with reflectors. All photographs were taken using a tripod-mounted Nikon FE2 with 24, 28, 35, 50, 55 Micro, 105, or 200mm Nikkor lens and a polarizing filter, if needed. The film used was Kodachrome 25, processed by Kodak.

Most of the photographs were taken in the New England gardens and orchards of Dr. Elwyn Meader, noted plant breeder, and Dr. E. Harry Boothby, whose hobby is gardening. Additional photographs were made at the farms and gardens of Norman White, Lionel Sevigny, and Bruce McMillan.